Freedom in the Workplace?

D0910937

Freedom in the Workplace?

GERTRUDE EZORSKY

CORNELL UNIVERSITY PRESS
ITHACA AND LONDON

BOWLING GREEN STATE UNIVERSITY LIBRARY

Copyright © 2007 by Cornell University

All rights reserved. Except for brief quotations in a review, this book, or
parts thereof, must not be reproduced in any form without permission in
writing from the publisher. For information, address Cornell University
Press, Sage House, 512 East State Street, Ithaca, New York 14850.

First published 2007 by Cornell University Press
First printing, Cornell Paperbacks, 2007

Printed in the United States of America

Library of Congress Cataloging-in-Publication Data

Ezorsky, Gertrude, 1926-
  Freedom in the workplace? / Gertrude Ezorsky.
      p. cm.
  Includes bibliographical references and index.
  ISBN 978-0-8014-4579-8 (cloth : alk. paper)—ISBN 978-0-8014-7369-2
(pbk.: alk. paper)
  1. Labor market—Moral and ethical aspects—United States. 2. Industrial
relations—Moral and ethical aspects—United States. 3. Quality of work
life—Moral and ethical aspects—United States. 4. Free enterprise—Moral
and ethical aspects—United States. 5. Liberty—Philosophy. I. Title.

  HD5724.E97 2007
  174'.40973—dc22

                                                          2007011000

Cornell University Press strives to use environmentally responsible
suppliers and materials to the fullest extent possible in the publishing of its
books. Such materials include vegetable-based, low-VOC inks and acid-
free papers that are recycled, totally chlorine-free, or partly composed of
nonwood fibers. For further information, visit our website at
www.cornellpress.cornell.edu.

Cloth printing   10 9 8 7 6 5 4 3 2 1
Paperback printing   10 9 8 7 6 5 4 3 2 1

PRINTED IN U.S.A.

For Eli

Contents

BOWLING GREEN STATE UNIVERSITY
DISCARDED
LIBRARY

Acknowledgments

Thanks for help from Lynn Chancer, Fred Michael, Stephen Shalom, Alan Wertheimer, Michael Hirsch, and Melinda Downey for her invaluable technical assistance.

Freedom in the Workplace?

Introduction

Most of us in the United States will spend our adult lives working for a living. During that time you will probably face important decisions. You might, for example, have to decide whether to accept a job offer or remain a full-time student. You might be conflicted about accepting a very low-paying service job just because it cannot be outsourced abroad. Or you might want to reject an offer because the employer does not provide health insurance or day care for your children. As an employee you might think twice about joining a labor union if your employer might fire you and it would be difficult to find another job in the current labor market.[1]

These decisions are made in what many thinkers (such as philosophers and social scientists) call a "free market." Of course, they acknowledge that our capitalist market is not completely free. Workers, for example, are prohibited by law from violating contracts with their employers, and employers are not legally free to discriminate by race and sex.

However, it is said by many thinkers that despite some limitations workers in our capitalist labor market enjoy great freedom. They are free to accept or refuse employer offers, and as employees they are free to remain in a job or quit.

It is true that some workers are fortunate enough financially to exercise such freedom. But a great many do not have that freedom. Put yourself in the position of these individuals:

1. An employee wants to blow the whistle on the owner of his plant who violates the Occupational Health and Safety Act (OSHA). The employee knows that conditions in the plant are harmful to those who work there, but he also knows that if he were to report the violation, the owner would (illegally) ensure that he is blacklisted in the industry. The worker's family depends on his wages, and he knows that he would have practically no chance of obtaining another position.

2. An impoverished, unemployed worker is offered a job that barely pays enough to feed himself and his family. The employer tells him, "Take it or leave it. Plenty of people would take this job." The unemployed person accepts the offer as the lesser evil to continued joblessness.

3. An ailing worker remains in her exhausting job because she and her diabetic children desperately need the health insurance the job provides.

Many thinkers would disagree as to whether the workers in these three cases are free or unfree. And how would the workers involved feel about their freedom or unfreedom?

Take the worker who is threatened with being blacklisted if he blows the whistle on his employer. Given that his family depends on his wages, is he free to blow that whistle? The worker would not think so and neither do I. Yet there are some philosophers who would disagree.

What of the impoverished, unemployed person who is offered a job that barely supports his family? The unemployed person surely would regard himself as unfree to refuse this offer and I agree with him. Yet the fact is many philosophers would regard him as free to do so.

The ailing worker who remains at her exhausting job for the health insurance she needs for her diabetic children surely believes that she is unfree to leave her position and I agree with her. Yet there are some philosophers and social scientists who would regard even her as enjoying the freedom found in capitalist society.

What workers themselves believe about their own freedom or unfreedom may not be the whole truth of the matter, but it is often closer to the truth than the views held by many theorists.

Important ethical issues are at work here. I shall suggest that the unfreedom of the three workers discussed above—and many like them—is wrongful. You may find yourself in situations where, contrary to some philosophers, you think of yourself as unfree and forced into a certain action. In the following pages, I shall explore such situations in depth. Let us begin with the meaning of freedom itself and then go on to forcing, using examples to show the reality of both.

Chapter I

The Obstacle Concept of Freedom

When is a person free or unfree to do (or not do) something?*

Let us follow the lead of Gerald C. McCallum Jr. He suggested that a person is free to do something (or not) when there are no obstacles, such as constraints, restrictions, or interfering conditions, which prevent her from doing something (or not). A person is unfree when there are such obstacles. (Hereafter, I refer to this as the *obstacle* concept.)[1] If the obstacle is not mentioned, it is usually understood from the context.

No one is simply free or unfree. One is free *from* an obstacle preventing someone from doing something (or not). One is unfree to do something (or not) because an obstacle prevents someone from doing it (or not).

---

* The concept of freedom and unfreedom developed here has no bearing on the metaphysical concept of free will.

Take the women production line workers at a Nabisco plant who were *unfree* to use the restroom. The obstacle to such use was a three-day suspension. Ordered to urinate in their clothes, they resorted to wearing diapers, incontinence pads, or less expensive toilet paper and Kotex—"protection" that is harmful when drenched with urine.

Workers at the plant, including men with serious kidney problems were *unfree* to use the restroom without permission. The obstacle to such use without first getting permission was suspension.[2]

Becoming Free

Suppose that the lack of day care at time t1 is an obstacle that renders a mother unfree to work. But day care becomes available to her at a later time, t2. Day care removes the obstacle to her working and she *becomes free* to do so. Her becoming free at time t2 implies that she was unfree before at time t1.

Suppose at time t1, a supervisor threatens a woman employee: if she complains about his sexual harassment he will not recommend her for the pay raise she badly needs to support her children. At time t1 the prospect of no pay raise is an obstacle that makes her unfree to complain. But at time t2, her union informs the employer about the supervisor's threat. Because of the union action on her behalf at time t2, she *becomes free* to complain about his sexual harassment. The union action *freed* her from the obstacle of the supervisor's threat.

Before 1964 blacks were unfree by law to sit at lunch counters with whites in the South. But in 1964 the Civil Rights Act freed them from that legal impediment. They became legally free to do so.

Active and Inactive Freedom and Unfreedom

A person's freedom and unfreedom shifts with time, as obstacles appear and disappear. For example, an obstacle to someone's living outside of a forced labor camp is created when she is brought into the camp. She is unfree to live outside the camp. If she is released the obstacle is removed and she becomes free to live on the outside.

It seems that, according to my view, I am free and unfree relative to countless obstacles. For example, travel to distant solar systems is physically impossible. Am I unfree to do so? Yet such travel has no relevance to my life. It seems odd to include it in a list of my unfreedoms.

Suppose such travel becomes physically possible. If I become free to engage in such travel at t2, I must have been unfree before at t1. Yet such freedom and unfreedom at t1 had no significance for me.

Let us distinguish two kinds of freedom and two kinds of unfreedom: *active* and *inactive*. My unfreedom now to travel to distant solar systems is inactive since such travel is not relevant to my life. (Relevance to my life includes relevance to my desires, wants, plans, and obligations.) If traveling to distant solar systems becomes physically possible and relevant to my life then my unfreedom to do so would become active. Of course, if I were now a space explorer who yearns to do the impossible—travel to distant solar systems—such travel, even if impossible, would be relevant to my life and I would be actively unfree to do so.

In what follows, unless otherwise specified, freedom and unfreedom are active.

Free and Unfree

One may be free and unfree at the same time to do a specific act relative to different obstacles. Suppose, for example, an employer asks his observant Jewish employee to work on the Sabbath. The worker may be free, relative to the nation's law, to work on the Sabbath but unfree relative to his religious prohibitions.

The fact that one may be free and unfree at the same time to do a specific action, relative to different obstacles is, as we shall see, important.

Kinds of Freedom and Unfreedom

A person may be physically unfree when her unfreedom is due to a purely physical obstacle. Thus a miner working in a cave is physically unfree to leave if the only exit is blocked by a naturally caused avalanche. My main focus in subsequent chapters, however, is not on physical but on *social freedom* and *social unfreedom*. In such cases the relevant obstacles significantly involve persons.

Whether social freedom or unfreedom is political, legal, or economic corresponds to the type of obstacle. Thus legal freedom to do something is the absence of legal obstacles to doing it. A worker is legally free to organize a union if there is no law such as the National Labor Relations Act prohibiting it. (Later I shall claim that the NLRA is a "toothless" law.)

Freedom as Morally Good

Is freedom always morally good?

Not always. The freedom of a murderer to escape, given the consequences of such freedom, is usually morally bad. The freedom of a person to express her opinions is usually morally good.

To determine whether a person's freedom is good or bad, we have to look at the context and consequences of such freedom.

Chapter II

Criticism of the Obstacle Concept of Freedom

Criticism of the obstacle concept of freedom might be made by two different kinds of philosophers, and I call their views Narrow Interference and Broad Interference.

Narrow Interference

Suppose that an immigrant worker is locked in a van by a human agent, called a "coyote," who is transporting him. The agent has made it *physically impossible* for the worker to leave. This kind of unfreedom in which a *person* makes it physically impossible for someone to do something is called *restraint*. According to Narrow Interference philosophers, restraint is the only kind of unfreedom.[1]

Broad Interference

Suppose an employee worked over forty hours and is therefore entitled to additional pay for overtime. Her employer threatens to fire her unless she alters her time card to show less than forty hours worked. Because she needs her job desperately in order to support her children, she agrees. (For discussion of actual cases of shaving time, see pp. 25–26.)

Note that it is not physically impossible for her to refuse to comply with her employer's threat. She is not restrained by anyone. Hence, according to Narrow Interference, she is free to say no.

But Broad Interference philosophers would disagree. They would claim that, since she is coerced—threatened—she is not free to say no.[2] According to Broad Interference philosophers, both restraint and coercion create unfreedom. Only restraint and coercion render individuals unfree.

How might these two kinds of philosophers—Narrow and Broad Interference—criticize the obstacle concept of freedom developed in the previous chapter? Let us focus on two cases:

First, at time t1 a miner, Joe, is trapped in a cave by an unforeseen, naturally caused avalanche that prevents him from leaving.

Second, at time t1, an impoverished farm worker, Nita, lacks the means—sufficient money—to support her family decently.

According to the obstacle concept, although the avalanche is a purely physical obstacle, it renders the miner unfree to leave. Note that this miner is not restrained as no person has made it physically impossible for him to leave the cave. Nor is he coerced (threatened) into remaining in the cave. Thus, according to both Narrow and Broad Interference, while at time t1 he is incapable of leaving, he is free to do so.

I suggest that contrary to both Narrow and Broad Interference, the trapped miner inside the cave, Joe, is unfree to leave at time t1. Here is why. Suppose that at time t2, the obstacle—the avalanche—to his leaving is removed. Hence, at time t2, he becomes free to leave. If he becomes free at t2, he must have been unfree to leave before at time t1 when the avalanche blocked his exit.

It may be argued that the trapped miner is neither free nor unfree. But in that case what are people doing when they *free* him? Note also that such purely physical unfreedom has moral implications. At least some people (rescue workers) are morally obligated to rescue him.

I conclude that, contrary to Narrow and Broad Interference, a purely physical obstacle may render a person unfree.

Let us turn now to the impoverished farm worker, Nita, who lacks the means—sufficient money—to support her family decently. Her poverty is not due to restraint or coercion—her employer is not threatening her—but to the low-wage policy of her employer's agribusiness. Also, Nita has no chance of a better job.

According to the obstacle concept, Nita is unfree to support her family decently. The obstacle to such support is lack of money. But a Narrow Interference philosopher would note that no person has restrained Nita—making it physically impossible for her to support her family. A Broad Interference philosopher would add that Nita is not coerced either since no person has threatened her. Hence, according to both Narrow and Broad Interference views, Nita is not unfree to support her family. They claim that lack of the means—sufficient money to support her family decently—does not exemplify unfreedom to do so.

Contrary to both Narrow and Broad Interference, I suggest that Nita is unfree to support her family. Here is why. At time t1, Nita cannot support them. But, suppose that at a later time t2, she gets a better job. Nita now has the means to support her family decently. This acquisition of the means at t2 to do so frees her, liberates her from her t1 poverty. At t2 she becomes free from her t1 poverty. Hence, contrary to Broad and Narrow Interference, she must have been unfree at t1 when—although not coerced or restrained—Nita lacked the means to support her family.

Let us turn now to other concepts of freedom that are different from the obstacle concept.

Moralized Concepts of Freedom

According to David Miller, "Constraints on freedom are those obstacles for which other human beings can be held *morally* responsible"[3] (emphasis added). However, as I have argued above, the miner trapped in the cave is rendered unfree to leave by an avalanche, although no human agent is morally responsible for this purely physical constraint on his freedom.

Robert Nozick holds a different moralized view of freedom: "Other people's actions place limits on one's available opportunities. Whether this makes one's resulting action non-voluntary [unfree] depends upon whether these others had the [moral] right to act as they did."[4]

However, as G. A. Cohen points out, Nozick's moralized account, "has the absurd upshot that if a criminal's imprisonment is morally justified, he is then not forced to be in prison."[5]

Freedom as Available Choice

Some philosophers argue that being free to do something means having an available choice to do it. Being unfree means having no available choice to do so.[6]

But suppose an individual is unfree by law at t1 to leave the country. A legal obstacle—a law—prevents her from leaving. If the legal obstacle is removed at t2 she becomes free to leave. Thus when the obstacle to her leaving is removed she acquires an available choice to leave.

Hence, if a person is free to do something she does have an available choice to do it. But she has that available choice because no obstacle prevents her from doing it.

Chapter III

Social Forcing

We are all familiar with the claim that a person is forced to do something (or not). Most people are forced to work because they need their pay. But there are different kinds of forcing.

Let us look at one type of forcing: *restraint*.

Restraint

Here is an actual case: poor young women worked over eighteen hours a day in a Los Angeles suburban sweatshop whose employer ordered the door locked and the yard encircled with a twelve-foot fence topped with razor wire. Hence, it was physically impossible for the women to leave. They had no choice but to remain inside.[1]

Generally speaking, when a person renders it physically impossible for another individual to do something (or not), then that individual is *restrained* by the person who did so.

Note that a human being—the employer in the sweat-shop case—is significantly involved in restraining these workers. Hence, the kind of forcing that this restraint case exemplifies is social forcing.

In what follows we shall focus our attention on cases of social forcing. In all of these cases, unless specified otherwise, the persons involved in doing or creating such forcing are able to choose not to do so.

Most philosophers agree that persons who are restrained are unfree. However, such agreement does not exist for a different kind of social forcing.

Social Forcing with Alternatives

Suppose a retail store supervisor, Phillip, tells Maria, an employee who suffers from chronic bronchitis, to accept lower pay for the same work or be reduced to a part-time assignment. As a part-time worker she would lose her health insurance, which she needs desperately. (Like temporary workers, part-time employees usually lack employer-sponsored health insurance.)[2] For Maria, the loss of health insurance is a greater evil than the alternative of reduced full-time pay. Hence, she complies with her boss's threat. The alternatives facing Maria are a lesser and a greater evil. She has no choice but to accept the lesser rather than the greater evil.

In cases of social forcing with alternatives, the individuals who are so forced are rational. They have only two alternatives because other alternatives are either worse than the ones they are facing or because the probability of achieving them is close to zero.

Recall that in the Los Angeles sweatshop, which exemplified restraint, it is physically impossible for the fenced-in young women to leave. In social forcing with alternatives, however, it is not physically impossible for these individuals to act on either alternative. Thus it is not physically impossible for Maria to refuse to accept the full-time work with reduced pay or to accept the transfer to part-time work.

There are two kinds of social forcing with alternatives. The first, *proposal forcing*, is illustrated by Maria's situation, in which she is forced to comply with her employer's threat rather than lose her health insurance.

A second kind is *systemic forcing*, which we shall examine later in chapter 5.

Proposal Forcing

In proposal forcing, an individual receives a proposal from an identifiable person, such as an employer (or employer's agent), which that individual is forced to accept as the lesser evil to a greater evil alternative. Proposal forcing can be either *strong* or *weak*.

Strong Proposal Forcing

The case of Maria illustrates *strong* proposal forcing because her alternatives are either transferring to part-time work without health insurance (the greater evil) or remaining full-time with reduced pay (the lesser evil). The greater evil results in an unacceptable level of hardship, so the individual is forced to accept the lesser evil. This type of strong proposal forcing is called a hardship case. Hardship refers to one of the following: serious adversity, privation, lack of access to necessary means of life, misery, suffering (mental or physical), harm or the risk of harm, or significant sacrifice for the self, dependents or loved ones. I shall, for the sake of simplicity (possibly despite ordinary language), include the prospect of death as a hardship.

Another type of strong proposal forcing case is the *rights* case.

Rights Cases

For example, an employer orders an employee, George, to "stop organizing a union in my plant or I'll cut your wages." George is resentful because he believes his employer has no right—moral or legal—to stop him from organizing a union, an act which is unrelated to his job performance. But George cannot support his children on lower wages; hence, he complies with his employer's threat. For George, compliance is the lesser evil compared with the greater evil of reduced wages.

Such threats in violation of the National Labor Relations Act (NLRA) are common in industry today (see page 21). I shall refer to both hardship and rights cases as lesser evil cases, in which a person such as George has no choice but to accept the alternative that exemplifies the lesser rather than the greater evil. I shall assume, unless otherwise specified, that in lesser evil cases people such as George have a right to accept the lesser evil. (Later in this chapter, I shall indicate the laws and policies that contribute to the vulnerability of workers to strong proposal forcing.)

Weak Forcing

In *weak* proposal forcing a person does not choose between two hardships. For example, a person from a well-off family is only weakly forced to work as a CEO because he wants the status. But being forced to work is not usually weak. For most people work is a hardship they endure because it is not as bad as the hardship of starvation.

There are, of course, varieties of forcing that are between strong and weak forcing, but we shall not pursue them. In the following, unless specified otherwise, we shall consider only strong forcing.

Coercion

Recall Maria, the retail worker afflicted with chronic bronchitis, who complies with her employer's threat to accept a cut in wages rather than transfer to part-time status, thereby losing her health insurance.

The kind of strong proposal forcing illustrated by this case is *coercion*. (A second kind—*forcing offer*—is described later in this chapter.)

What is coercion?

Coercion is typically exemplified either explicitly or implicitly (as in an order or law) by a threat. When the employer threatens Maria, she is aware that her employer intends to harm her by transferring her to part-time status unless she accepts lower full-time wages. Let us assume that her employer is not bluffing and the threat is successful. In that case, Maria is coerced into compliance by her employer. Coercion always exemplifies social forcing since it is a *person* who makes the threats.*

An actual example of coercion is worth noting. Marvin Gaddy, an employee in the film division at the Olin Corporation for more than twenty years, "knew—even though the company never told him—[that] the process [he was using] was harming his fellow workers: 'People would act

---

* Note that a threat is different from a warning. When John warns Bob, "If you continue to drink so much, you'll become an alcoholic," his intent may be to help him.

real unusual, get headaches and think they were getting the flu. After a few overdoses, the nightmares would start coming on them.' Management did not tell Gaddy or any of the other workers that their exposure … could cause nerve damage. . . . When Gaddy and his coworkers complained to the company, management's response was 'We don't need you. If you don't enjoy your job, then go home.'"[3] The workers were coerced into not complaining because they knew that if they complained again they would be fired.

Employment at Will

A legal doctrine that has contributed to the vulnerability of workers to coercion is Employment at Will. This doctrine was stated by the U.S. Supreme Court in *Coppage v. Kansas* (1915): "An employer may discharge his employee for any reason, or for no reason" (see appendix).[4]

Since *Coppage*, federal and state laws have created a number of exceptions to Employment at Will. The National Labor Relations Act (1935) prohibits discharge for union organizing (see appendix). More recent exceptions are provided by laws that ban discrimination against minorities, women, and the disabled, or prohibit discharge for whistle-blowing.

Occupational Safety and Health

As Beth Shulman notes, "federal law guarantees the right of all workers to a safe and healthy workplace [see appendix].

But low-wage workers face unsafe and unhealthy conditions every day. . . . Workers who cooperate with OSHA or speak out against hazardous working conditions" are vulnerable to illegal coercion. They face the threat of years of blacklisting and unemployment for doing so.[5]

McWane, one of the largest manufacturers of cast-iron water and sewer pipes, for example, has by far the worst safety record in an industry that has one of the highest injury rates in the United States. But workers who protest dangerous (and illegal) safety conditions "are often 'bullseyed'—marked for termination."[6]

Coercion that involves occupational health and safety is also evident in this person's circumstances:

> Earl Craig … is on his knees for eight hours straight, starting at 11 p.m., waxing and cleaning the floors of a 50,000-square-foot supermarket. He has a burning sensation under his knees, and his shoulders and arms ache constantly. He has had to work nineteen days straight without a break because his employer hasn't trained anyone else to do the job. *He can't ask for time off because he fears they will fire him.*[7] [Emphasis added.]

Union Organizing
Union organizing in most industries is protected legally by the National Labor Relations Act (see appendix). But many union organizers often refer to this law as "toothless"

because the penalty for employer violation of the NLRA is minimal and cases can drag on for years before settlement:

> There is the case of Avondale shipyard in New Orleans, in which the NLRB found that the company violated the workers' rights to organize by transferring union supporters to more difficult and dirtier jobs, by threatening to close the yard if a majority of workers voted for the union, by interrogating and spying on union supporters, by firing twenty-eight union supporters, and by threatening to fire other union supporters. *In spite of these flagrant violations of the law, it was not until eight years later that bargaining began*, and it occurred only because Avondale was sold to Litton Industries, who agreed to abide by the Board's ruling.[8] [Emphasis added.]

Employers also threaten to outsource jobs, sending them out of the country to low-wage areas, such as Mexico, India, or China, to prevent union organizing or to weaken the union's position in negotiations when issues such as wages, health insurance, or pensions are on the table. Nancy Holmstrom notes that when business interests organized for the passage of NAFTA, which promised to make it easier to outsource to Mexico, they were perfectly frank about using the relocation threat in negotiations with labor.[9]

Kim Moody states that in 2004 while only 8 percent of private sector workers are unionized, "fully 39 percent of the jobs being shifted out of the United States were from unionized facilities."[10] And John Sweeney, president of the AFL-CIO, noted, "Companies illegally threaten to close up shop if workers want to unionize, and in 25 percent of unionization drives they illegally fire workers who support a union."[11] According to a Cornell University study, "more than half of all employers across a wide range of industries use these threats [of job loss and plant closing] as part of their anti-union strategy."[12]

The journalist Bob Herbert reported on conditions in the Smithfield Pork processing plant in Tar Heel, North Carolina, and efforts to organize a union there. "The work," he said, "is often brutal beyond imagining." According to one employee, you work fast because the machine shoots hogs out at you constantly. At the end you can have "all this blood dripping down on you, all these feces and stuff just hanging off of you. It's a terrible environment." Herbert goes on to report:

> Workers are cut by the flashing, slashing knives ... [and] are hurt sliding and falling on floors and stairs that are slick with blood, guts and a variety of fluids ...
>
> The [United Food and Commercial Workers Union] lost votes to organize the plant in 1994 and 1997, but the results of those elections were thrown out by the National Labor Relations Board after the judge found that Smithfield had prevented the union from holding

fair elections … [and] had engaged in myriad "egregious" violations of federal labor law, including threatening, intimidating and firing workers involved in the organizing effort, and beating up a worker "for engaging in union activities."[13]

After mining and construction, work by nursing home aides is the next most dangerous job in the United States. In understaffed nursing homes aides work long hours and are often injured lifting patients and moving equipment. To combat low pay, long hours, and health and safety hazards, they have tried to organize unions, but Human Rights Watch found "a pattern of threats, intimidation, and firings of nursing home workers trying to form and join unions and of employers' refusal to bargain when workers succeeded."[14]

At the Palm Garden Nursing Home, for example, "company officials unlawfully threatened loss of benefits and wage cuts if workers chose union representation. With such low wages, many employees were eligible for food stamps and needed assistance with English-language forms. One powerful threat was to stop helping workers fill out food stamp applications."[15]

Shaving Time
Doctoring employee records that show hours worked is practiced by some companies to illegally reduce the pay of workers.

Employees are threatened with dismissal if they refuse to sign time cards that indicate fewer hours than they actually worked. Employers are required by law to pay time and half to workers who put in over forty hours in one week. But managers are told to eliminate entries that would require time and a half pay. Although some of these managers are offered bonuses, they face the implicit threat of termination if they refuse.[16]

Coercion of Immigrants

I will look at two kinds of immigrant workers who are most often subject to coercion: farm laborers and domestics (nannies and maids).

Farm workers, many of whom are immigrants, are "the most ignored, exploited and vulnerable population in this country." But "relatively few complain" to government agencies "for fear of losing their job or being deported, according to a 2000 General Accounting Office report."[17]

Farm workers believe that one complaint would cost them their job. According to one farm worker, "No one will say a bad word about their job or [company] housing in front of a stranger or even an acquaintance."[18]

A Justice Department official described the dreadful conditions of immigrant farm laborers in southern Florida as "ground zero for modern slavery." A U.S. Border Patrol agent stated, "There's no escape … [the employers will] find you. And heaven help you when they do."[19]

In addition to their virtual incarceration, adolescent farm workers are likely to be the most pesticide-exposed subgroup in the United States. A Human Rights Watch report gave this example:

> On June 27, 1997, seventeen-year-old migrant farmworker José Antonio Casillas collapsed and died while riding his bike near his home in rural Utah. Emergency workers found white foam streaming from his nose. According to José's uncle, the day before he died the boy had been soaked with pesticide sprayed from a tractor; a week earlier he had also been sprayed, while working in a peach orchard. After the second spraying he showed symptoms of severe pesticide poisoning, including vomiting, sweating, diarrhea and headaches. He had received no training from his employer regarding pesticide dangers and the symptoms of exposure, and reportedly slept in his pesticide-soaked clothing the night before his death.

An outreach worker told Human Rights Watch that when workers with blisters and pesticide-related health issues *"confronted their farm labor contractor or employer they were fired—gone the next day"*[20] (emphasis added).

Women farm workers, especially young ones, are often victims of sexual harassment. They are "subjected routinely to sexual advances by farm labor contractors and field supervisors. If they refuse, they—and members of their

family—face [threats of] retaliation in the form of discharge, blacklisting, and even physical assault and rape."[21]
When one young woman reported hearing about another
woman who had been raped by her employer but did nothing about it, she explained the victim's reticence: "He's the
boss."[22]

Domestics are another group who face coercion, and
their numbers are increasing. One reason their numbers
are increasing is this: Developed countries and international lending organizations often prescribe drastic preconditions for loans to third world countries, such as freezing
wages and cutting basic social services. As a consequence of
such policies, poor women are often forced to leave for the
United States in order to earn money for their families. A
growing number of these women are abused in the homes
where they work as nannies or maids. Typically, if they
complain, *they are coerced by their employers who threaten to
send them home or turn them over to the police*. Women who
flee abusive situations are, according to law, immediately
considered out of status, ineligible for other employment
and liable to deportation.[23] Human Rights Watch provides this assessment of the conditions under which many
domestics work:

> In the most egregious cases of exploitation, employ-
> ers feel free to create living and working conditions

equivalent to indentured servitude. Numerous cases have surfaced of live-in migrant domestic workers—both documented and undocumented—working over one hundred hours per week, from early morning until late at night six or seven days a week with no holidays, receiving compensation far below the national minimum wage if they are paid at all …

Yeshehareg Teferra, an Ethiopian woman, worked in Silver Spring, Maryland, for eight years for an Ethiopian staff member of the International Monetary Fund. She worked seven days a week, thirteen hours a day with no days off during the eight years. She received total compensation of $1,060 during that time-the equivalent of three cents an hour. Teferra said she was ordered not to speak with people outside the family; was required to ask permission prior to leaving the apartment; and was slapped, choked, and verbally abused when she complained of her treatment.[24]

Let us turn now to another kind of strong proposal forcing that I call Forcing Offers.

Forcing Offers

Suppose an employer offers unemployed and impoverished Steve a job in a dangerous plant area. The employer indicates no intent to harm or to adversely affect Steve if he refuses. Indeed the employer may say, "Take it or leave it. There are plenty of people who would accept this offer." Even if Steve is the only candidate and the employer's purpose is to get Steve to accept, since the employer is not threatening Steve, he is not coercing him.

Although the employer is not coercing him, Steve is nevertheless strongly forced to accept the employer's proposal as the lesser evil. For Steve, the alternative of unemployment is the greater evil, since it imposes greater hardship on him and his family. He has no alternative but to accept the offer.

The employer's offer exemplifies a *forcing offer*. As in coercion, the person who receives a forcing offer is strongly forced to accept the lesser evil. Also like coercion, a forcing offer can violate a worker's rights. Suppose an employer says to an applicant, "The job is yours if you agree not to organize a union." This offer is a violation of the National Labor Relations Act, but the applicant who needs the job desperately is forced to agree.

Let us look at some actual cases of forcing offers. During the Depression unemployment was at a record high. A midwestern gypsum plant worker recounted that when employees reported for work, the manager offered them lower pay for the same job they were doing before. Their wages would be reduced from 30–45 cents to 25 cents an hour. The plant manager said, "If you want to work, you can; if you don't, I can get plenty of men at that price."[25]

A foundry in Texas supplies a more recent example: "It is said that only the desperate seek work at Tyler Pipe, … a dim, dirty, hellishly hot place where men are regularly disfigured by amputations and burns, … where some workers urinate in their pants because their bosses refuse to let them step away from the manufacturing line for even a few moments."

Rolan Hoskin was from "the ranks of the desperate." A master electrician, Hoskin suffered severe economic problems and was forced to accept an entry-level, grave-yard shift job maintaining the conveyor belts at Tyler Pipe. Despite federal safety regulations, the belt he was working on was not shut down while he worked on it. "He was found on his knees. His left arm had been crushed. . . . His head had been pulled between belt and rollers. His skull had split."[26]

A forcing offer can also take the form of what is called a payday loan. Some payday lenders offer loans against a worker's next paycheck for a fee that annually exceeds 300–400 percent and in some cases up to four digits. Such loans may be renewed again and again for the same fee. Low-wage workers, unable to meet living expenses, may be forced to accept such usurious loan offers. One such person was a partly disabled taxi driver. Living at the edge of her income, she was unable to pay a $1,900 hospital bill. Hence, with poor credit she was forced "in desperation" to turn to a payday loan company and accept a loan. Unable to repay because of her income, her loan was renewed and soon she owed an enormous debt.[27]

Forcing offers of farm work are often made to adolescents. Although farm labor is "low-paid, exhausting, … and often dangerous," thirteen- to fifteen-year-olds from extremely poor families in rural areas are *forced to* accept offers of farm labor because no other work is available.[†] "Twelve-hour days are routine, as are six and seven-day work weeks. . . . Those who live near towns leap at the chance to work instead at a fast-food restaurant or supermarket."[28]

Recall the policies described earlier in this chapter of developed countries and international lending organizations that impose drastic preconditions for loans to third world countries, such as cutting basic social services and freezing wages. Because of such economic policies poor women are often *forced to accept offers* to work as nannies, thousands of miles away from their home.[‡] They make a heartbreaking decision to leave their own children—possibly for years—

[†] Reports of children as young as four or five years old working alongside their parents are not uncommon.

[‡] In a thoughtful article, Norman Daniels seems to suggest that the type of case described above—in which as a result of drastic economic

to take care of other people's children and so that they can send money to their families.[29]

Differences between Coercion and Forcing Offers

I have argued that in both coercion and forcing offers the worker's situation is relevantly similar. In both situations the worker is strongly forced to accept an employer's proposal as the lesser evil. In both cases they can say, "I had no choice."

There are relevant differences, however, between forcing offers and coercion. Let us illustrate them by considering two cases, one of coercion, the other of a forcing offer.

Coercion: An employer threatens his employee Raymond, "Take a new (awful) work assignment or I'll fire you." Raymond's circumstances are such that no better

politics, third world women accept forcing offers to work as nannies abroad—should be called "quasi-coercive." He writes: "Let us call a proposal *quasi-coercive* if it imposes or depends on a restriction of someone's alternatives in a way that is unfair or unjust; that is, a just or fair social arrangement would involve a range of options for the individual both broader than and strongly preferred to the range in the proposal situation." However, since such cases exemplify forcing offers, I would rather describe them as forcing offers rather than quasi-coercive proposals. See Norman Daniels, "Does OSHA Protect Too Much?" in *Moral Rights in the Workplace,* ed. Gertrude Ezorsky (Albany: State University of New York Press, 1987), 54.

job is available. For Raymond unemployment is a greater evil than enduring the new work assignment. Hence, he is forced to comply with his employer's threat. He can say: "I had no other choice."

Forcing offer: A different employer makes a forcing offer to a jobless worker, Vicky, who is almost destitute because of unemployment. The offer is the same kind of awful job proposed to Raymond in the coercion case. Also, as in the coercion case, no better position is available for Vicky and continued unemployment is the greater evil. As in the coercion case Vicky is forced to accept the job as the lesser evil. As in the coercion case she can say, "I had no choice."

The cases of Raymond and Vicky demonstrate the similarities between coercion (Raymond's case) and a forcing offer (Vicky's case). But there are also relevant differences between them. In the coercion case Raymond is forced both by his employer and his circumstances such as the unemployment market. Hence, he complies with his employer's threat. In the forcing offer case, however, Vicky is forced *only* by circumstance, such as the employment market that she faces. As I indicated earlier, the employer might say, "Take it or leave it. I can get plenty of people for this job."

In the coercion case the employer who threatens Raymond indicates that he *intends* to harm Raymond by imposing the greater hardship—dismissing him—unless he complies with his threat. By contrast, in the forcing offer case, the employer has indicated *no intention* of imposing a greater hardship on Vicky who is already unemployed.

When any offer, forcing or not, is accepted, we may assume that it was accepted because it made the person better off than he or she was before receiving it. That is why, as David Zimmerman states, workers accepting a genuine offer generally do "want to move from the pre-proposal [before the offer] to the proposal situation [when the offer is made]."[30]

Hence, generally speaking, when workers accept offers, they would prefer not to return to the preproposal situation since they are better off accepting the proposal. This is also true of a forcing offer. Vicky would not prefer to be back in the preproposal situation since, by acceptance of the awful offer, she is less badly off; hence, better off. She at least has a job. By contrast, Raymond, who is coerced by his employer into agreeing to the awful work assignment, would prefer to be back in the preproposal situation, before being threatened, when he had a better work assignment.

I have claimed that in both the coercion and forcing offer cases the worker is forced to accept the employer's proposal. In the coercion case, acceptance by workers such as Raymond is given against his will since acceptance makes him worse off than before the employer's proposal. But in the forcing offer case, Vicky, the unemployed worker's acceptance is not given against her will. Hence, as miserable as the work is, it is the lesser evil to unemployment. She wants the job because it makes her less badly off. As some say, "A dreadful job is better than none."[31]

According to Joseph Raz, if Vicky is forced to accept this job, she must regret the circumstances that force her to do so.[32] But I suggest that although she regrets being in that circumstance—her near destitution—she does not regret receiving the offer of the job since it improves her circumstances. Nevertheless in a forcing offer—as in coercion—the worker's acceptance may be accompanied by outrage or resentment against her employer for taking advantage of her.

Consider a person who works for a U.S. company in Haiti. She lives in a malaria- and dysentery-ridden hovel and is offered a job at the going rate of 28 cents an hour. Suppose she learns that the CEO of the U.S. company earns about $10,000 an hour. It is surely reasonable that she would feel that *her employer is taking advantage of her*.[33]

Throffers

According to the welfare to work law of 1996 (see appendix), welfare recipients are *threatened* with the loss of cash assistance if they refuse an *offer* of any kind of work without good cause. This combined threat and offer exemplifies a throffer: an offer becomes a forcing offer when it is combined with a threat.

Recall the religious worker who is free relative to the nation's law to work on the Sabbath but unfree relative to his religion. He is free relative to the absence of a legal obstacle but unfree relative to the presence of a religious obstacle. Hence, he is not *just* free or *just* unfree. He is *both* free and unfree.

I claim that in both coercion and forcing offer cases the worker also is *both free and unfree.* In the coercion case described earlier, Raymond is threatened by his employer: take a new (awful) job assignment or be fired. Raymond complies with the threat since unemployment is the greater hardship and therefore the greater evil. Raymond can say that he had no choice but to comply.

In the forcing offer case, Vicky receives a forcing offer of the same kind of awful job. But continued unemployment is the greater hardship—the greater evil—for her and her family. Hence, she has no choice but to accept the forcing offer.

In the coercion case Raymond is *free*, relative to any obstacle that *prevents* his compliance with his employer's threat (there is no such obstacle). But he is *unfree* relative to the obstacle of the prospect of future unemployment if he refuses. Because of that obstacle he is forced to comply with his employer's threat.

The same contrast of freedom and unfreedom holds for the forcing offer case. Vicky, an unemployed worker, is free relative to the absence of an obstacle which would prevent her from accepting the employer's offer. But relative to the obstacle of continued unemployment, she is unfree to refuse.

Hence, in the coercion and forcing offer cases these workers are *both* free and unfree.

A Puzzle about Unfreedom

I have claimed that when threatened by coercion, a person (relative to the obstacle of a greater evil) is unfree.

Gerald Dworkin notes a puzzle about that person's presumed unfreedom in coercion "that bothered people."

"If one thought of a person as acting *freely* when he did what he *wanted* to do, ... then why should threats be thought to deprive him of freedom?" (emphasis added). He thinks that by complying he would be better off. Since he did what he "*wanted*" he "*acted freely*."

There are two resolutions of this puzzle.

The first is Gerald Dworkin's. When someone interferes with a person's status quo situation, that person resents "acting merely in order to retain a status quo against the interference of another agent." Milton, the employer, has interfered with Eugene's status quo situation (being employed). Eugene complies in order to maintain his status quo of employment. Hence he is unfree.[34]

The second resolution is Gertrude Ezorsky's. Two senses of want—a strong and a weak—should be distinguished. When a friend asks you for a loan you are not *forced* to comply. Hence, you *want in the strong sense* to lend him the money.

But Eugene is *forced* to comply with Milton's threat (the alternative of joblessness is worse). Hence, Eugene *wants in the weak sense* to comply with Milton's threat.

CHAPTER IV

Some Moral Issues of Proposal Forcing

Let us focus on the following coercion and forcing offer cases.

Coercion: A worker, Jack, is ordered by his employer to transfer from one area of the plant to one that is dangerous. The employer threatens to reduce Jack to part-time work if he refuses the transfer. As a part-time employee, Jack would lose his health insurance, which he and his family need desperately. Hence, Jack has no choice but to accept the transfer as the lesser hardship.

Forcing Offer: Unemployed Irene is forced to accept the offer of a job that is exhausting, low paying, and lacking in benefits such as health insurance. But she has no alternative of a better job and without a job she cannot support her family. Irene has no choice but to accept the miserable job as the lesser hardship. She is forced to accept the employer's offer.

In both the coercion and the forcing offer cases, the employer's proposal is wrong. Recall that these employers can afford to pay benefits such as health insurance. Although Jack and Irene have the right to accept it, they are wronged by the employer who profits by taking unfair advantage of their vulnerability when they have no choice but to accept the employer's proposal.

Let us look now at the moral issues in some strong forcing cases that are more complicated.

Forced to Commit a Grave Moral Offense?

In cases where there is disagreement as to whether an individual would commit a grave moral offense by complying with a proposal, there is also disagreement as to whether the individual is really forced to accept this proposal.

Consider these cases:

First, suppose that an employer threatens his employee, an orthodox impoverished Jew, "Work on the Sabbath or I'll fire you."

Second, suppose an employer offers an orthodox impoverished Jewish candidate a job if he would agree to work on the Sabbath.

Are these orthodox Jewish workers forced in either case to violate the Sabbath?

One can imagine an orthodox Jew saying to both of them, "You are not forced to work on the Sabbath (except to save a life). Doing so is utterly wrong. You have no right to do so." But one could also imagine their spouses disagreeing, "But he is forced to work on the Sabbath because he is morally obligated to support his family. Hence his working on the Sabbath is not wrong."*

As discussed earlier, some employers order managers to doctor their employee's records of hours worked to illegally reduce their wages. Workers are threatened with being fired if they refuse to cooperate. While in some cases the managers are offered bonuses if they obey company orders, they face the threat of dismissal if they refuse to obey the "shaving time" order and coerce an employee into accepting less than the pay to which they are entitled.

Such coercion by a manager in order to collect a bonus for himself is surely wrong. But what of the cases in which the manager himself is coerced by the employer—threatened with dismissal—unless he coerces the worker into shaving his time?

The employer's coercion of the manager is surely wrong. But is the manager's coercion of the worker—which the employer has ordered—also wrong?

I suggest that the manager's coercion of the worker is also wrong. However, given that the manager is himself

* Alan Wertheimer criticized an earlier version of this section, "Forced to Commit a Grave Moral Offense?" in correspondence. The above text is a revision that responds to his criticism.

coerced, his blame is considerably reduced, possibly to zero. Since his coercion of the worker is illegal, the manager's legal penalty for his offence should be substantially reduced. His being coerced to coerce constitutes a strong mitigating circumstance.

Suppose that an employer offers unemployed workers jobs that are so low paying that they must turn to public assistance, such as food stamps. But in this case the employer cannot improve his offers without going bankrupt. Moreover, the employer has taken measures such as reducing the pay of managers and highly paid workers to avoid bankruptcy. In that case, the employer's forcing offers are not wrong.

In union-organized enterprises, workers must accept requirements that have been negotiated with the employer. Thus a worker who believes in an open shop—where workers have no representation—is forced to accept such requirements.

In a closed shop workers must be union members in order to be hired. In a union shop they must join the union. In an agency shop they are not required to join the union, but they must pay a fee equivalent to union dues.

A worker who believes in an "open shop" is forced to act contrary to his beliefs if he is to work in any of these union-organized shops. Is he wrongly coerced into doing what he believes violates his rights?

I suggest that such "coercion" is not really wrong. If this worker were exempted from the union requirements described above, he would unfairly enjoy the benefits that the union has negotiated and fought for. These include such benefits as increased wages, health insurance, and the "just cause" requirement found in most union contracts that prevent an employer from firing or disciplining employees without just cause. If an employer fires or disciplines an employee without just cause, the union is there to represent him in a grievance for contract violation. Thus the union requirements imposed on the worker who believes in an open shop are fair and reduce the coercive power of employers. Hence, such conditions are not really wrong.

Moral Obligations of Victims of Strong Forcing

Let us focus on these cases:

Coercion: An employer threatens his workers, "Take a significant wage cut and less health insurance or I'll move my plant." If the workers' wages were significantly reduced, they would urgently need public assistance such as food stamps to feed their families. They are also dependent on their employer-sponsored health insurance. Hence, they are forced to comply with their employers' threat.

Forcing Offer: Unemployed workers are forced to accept jobs that do not pay health insurance and offer such low wages that they would urgently need food stamps to support their families.

Suppose now that in both the coercion and forcing offer cases, the workers involved were required to agree to remain in their positions under the conditions they had accepted for at least one year. However, suppose that in both of these cases, before the year is up, each worker receives an offer from another employer of a job that pays enough to support their families decently and provides them with health insurance.

Do these workers have a moral obligation in each case to refuse the offer of a decent job because they agreed to stay for one year? In a coercion case the worker is not morally required to live up to his agreement. As Alan Wertheimer states, an "agreement lacks its normal moral force if it is coerced."[1]

But Wertheimer applies his claim only to coerced agreements. I suggest, however, that the worker who accepted the forcing offer is also not morally required to live up to this agreement. Both workers were strongly forced to accept the position for a one-year term as the lesser hardship to refusing. The employer's proposal was wrong and these vulnerable workers had no choice but to agree.

The agreement loses its normal moral force in the forcing offer case as well as a coercion case. The workers who are victims of these forcing offers or coerced agreements are not morally obligated to refuse the offer of decent jobs.

In a suggestive article, Jeffrie G. Murphy makes a similar claim: "Even if there is no duress or coercion and loss of freedom in that sense, a contract or agreement may still fail to generate an obligation if it is unconscionable—i.e., agreed to in circumstances unfair to one of the parties."[2]

Moral Differences between Coercion and Forcing Offers

As I have mentioned, there are relevant moral *similarities* between coercion and forcing offers. In both cases vulnerable workers are taken advantage of unfairly by proposals that, because of their desperate situation, they are forced to accept. I shall now suggest some moral *differences* between coercion and forcing offers.

Coercion: An employer orders an employee, Mark, to take a new position in the plant. The new assignment is much worse than Mark's current assignment. However, his circumstances are such that no better job is available. For Mark and his family, unemployment is the greater hardship—the greater evil—while the miserable job assignment is the lesser hardship—the lesser evil. Hence, he is forced by his employer and his circumstances to accept his employer's proposal. He can say, "I had no choice but to comply with my boss's threat."

Forcing Offer: A different employer makes a forcing offer to Annie, an unemployed worker, of the same kind of job. As in the coercion case above, no better position is available, and unemployment is the greater hardship for her and her family. As in the coercion case she is forced to accept the job as the lesser evil. (She and her family are almost destitute.) As in the coercion case she can say, "I had no choice but to accept."

In both of the two cases described above—the forcing offer and coercion—a worker is forced to choose between a lesser hardship—the awful position—or a greater hardship—unemployment.

Let us now focus only on the fact that one is a coercion and the other a forcing offer. What *moral difference* does that make?

While in both cases, as I have claimed, the employer's proposal is wrong, nevertheless, I shall argue that in the coercion case the employer's proposal is wrong to a greater degree, and the employer is more blamable than in the forcing offer case.

In the coercion case, the employer indicates his *intent* to harm Mark by transfer to an awful job. Whereas in the forcing offer case the employer indicates no such adverse *intent*. Indeed, in the forcing offer case the employer may say to Annie, "Take it or leave it. Plenty of people would take this job." Hence, in the coercion case, given the employer's intent to harm or adversely affect Mark if he refuses, the employer's proposal is wrong to a greater degree, and the employer is more blamable than in the forcing offer case.

In the coercion case Mark becomes worse off by complying with the employer's threat than he was before receiving it, when he had a better work assignment. But in the forcing offer case, Annie becomes less badly off by accepting the job, awful as it is, than she was before receiving it, when she had no job at all. Hence, a forcing offer is not as wrong as coercion.

Chapter V

Systemic Forcing

I have focused on social forcing cases in which a worker receives a proposal from a human being, an employer. But there are some cases, which I call *systemic forcing*, in which the worker receives no proposal yet, as in proposal forcing, is forced to choose a lesser over a greater evil. Human beings have created and maintain these systems, so humans are still significantly involved in these workers being forced to act. Hence, such forcing is social forcing.

Let us look at examples of four such systems: day care, transportation, pension, and health care.[1]

Day Care

Because adequate day care for their children is often not available, many low-wage workers are forced to quit or refuse a job offer. They do not qualify for unemployment insurance to tide them over because under most unemployment laws, lack of adequate day care is not an acceptable reason for quitting or refusing a job.

At fault is the day care system in the United States, as well as our country's unemployment insurance system, which forces many low-wage workers to leave work to care for their children.[2]

Transportation

Low-wage workers may be forced to refuse a job offer, since buses and subways often do not reach poor neighborhoods or stop running at night. "For many, taking or losing a job comes down to whether a ride [or affordable housing] is available."[3]

Because there was no public transportation system in her area, a certified nursing assistant who earned $350 every two weeks for working the night shift, was forced to pay someone to drive her to work. When there was no ride available she walked several miles at night to her job. She was afraid of being fired if she missed a day's work.[4]

Pension

Consider a worker who labors under the stress of increasingly difficult conditions, which are found in one industry after another. She may be forced to leave her job thereby

losing the full pension that she needs for her family, because she can no longer tolerate such stress. But losing that
pension is the lesser evil to continuing to endure the working conditions that come with her job.

Kim Moody gives an example from one industry:
"Telecommunications workers ... are taking the early
retirement ... because they know they cannot work much
longer. In industry after industry, the combination of
intensified work, longer hours, rotating shift work, and job
insecurity is taking an unrecorded toll on the health and
safety of workers."[5]

Health Care

Over forty million Americans have no health insurance.
Eight out of ten are in working families without employer-
sponsored health plans or government-sponsored payment
for primary care. They rely on emergency rooms for their
primary care. Hence, they may be forced to choose between continued illness, such as the flu, and very expensive
emergency room care, which puts them in debt for years.
A worker who had no health insurance stated that her last
visit to an emergency room cost her $1,000. She is still try-
ing to pay off that debt.[6]

Health care plans (government- or employer-sponsored)
that exclude many low-wage workers from primary care

are at fault. As mentioned previously, part-time workers usually receive no employer-sponsored health care. In the case of an adjunct lecturer, she was entitled to health care but had to endure great hardship to receive it: "'As an adjunct I got no maternity leave after my baby was born. I had to return immediately to work and I had to teach two courses so I would not lose my health care. I felt torn apart but I had no choice.' [The mother] wanted to spend precious time with her newborn but she was afraid to lose her health insurance, just when she needed it most. So she went back to work."[7]

Employed parents whose children have serious illnesses (such as diabetes) that require an exhausting regimen of care may be forced to stay on their jobs, which intensifies their burden, because it provides health insurance. For these families, "losing [health] insurance is a life-or-death situation."[8] At fault is a system (government or employer) that excludes parents from health insurance if they stay home to care for their sick children.

In these cases of systemic forcing, workers are forced to accept the lesser evil. No obstacle prevents them from accepting the lesser evil; hence, they are free to accept it. But relative to the obstacle of the greater evil, they are forced; hence, they are unfree to accept it. Each one is both free and unfree, but as forced and therefore unfree, unfreedom is more significant, as it is in proposal forcing.

CHAPTER VI

Criticism of Social Forcing Analysis

Recall the criticism of my analysis of freedom and un-freedom according to Narrow and Broad Interference views. Now we shall consider criticism of my social forcing analysis.

Coercion and Coercive or Forcing Offer

First, let us review the essential differences between coercion and forcing offers.

Coercion: Recall the employer who threatens Mark by ordering him to move to an awful assignment or be fired. Mark accepts the bad assignment as the lesser evil to unemployment.

Forcing Offer: An employer offers the same kind of job in a dangerously polluted area to a destitute unemployed worker, Annie, who accepts the forcing offer as the lesser evil to continued destitution.

Note the similarities between the two cases. Both workers are taken advantage of and are forced to accept the employer's proposal, but the two cases are also relevantly different. First, in the coercion case, the employer intends to impose an adverse consequence on Mark (dismissal) if he rejects the proposal to move to an awful work area. The employer who makes a forcing offer to Annie, meanwhile, has no such intent. She is already unemployed.

Second, while in both the coercion and forcing offer cases, the workers accept the employer's proposal, their situations upon acceptance are relevantly different. Mark, the coerced worker is worse off than just before the employer's proposal, when he had a better work assignment. But Annie, who receives a forcing offer, is less badly off and hence better off than just before the employer's proposal since a miserable job is not as bad as continued destitution.

Now let us consider three cases: a profit-seeking butcher, a greedy lifesaver, and a lecherous millionaire. The profit-seeking butcher raises the price of meat unfairly to a customer who is dependent on him for meat, which is essential to her health. The greedy lifesaver offers to rescue a drowning person if she promises him a ten-thousand-dollar reward. The lecherous millionaire offers to pay for a child's expensive life-saving operation that his mother cannot pay for on the condition that the mother become his mistress for a period.

The Profit-Seeking Butcher

The butcher raises his price to a customer who is (1) dependent on the butcher for meat, which is (2) essential to his health, and (3) is being charged an exploitative and unfair price.

According to Harry Frankfurt, given these three conditions, the butcher is threatening his customer.[1]

My response: The butcher is not threatening his customer. He is making a forcing offer to him. Here is why. Suppose the customer complies with what Frankfurt considers a threat and pays the higher price. In that case, he has been *coerced* by the butcher. But this customer has not been coerced. In a coercion case (but not a forcing offer) A intends to impose an adverse consequence on B. However, the butcher has no such intent. He is not out to get this customer and can say, "Take it or leave it. Plenty of people are ready to pay this price."

Moreover, a coerced person is worse off after accepting the threat proposal than just before he received it. But the customer who accepts the butcher's higher price offer is better off than just before he received it. He now has the meat he needs badly. Being better off than before is true of a forcing offer, not of coercion. It is true that the customer is forced to accept the higher price, but such forcing is true also of a forcing offer.

The Greedy Lifesaver

Suppose Marvin offers to save drowning Mildred if and only if she promises him a reward of ten thousand dollars. Mildred always keeps her promises.

According to Vinit Haksar, Marvin's offer is a *coercive offer* because he is taking unfair advantage of Mildred. Although Marvin is forcing Mildred, he is not threatening her. If he were threatening her, Mildred would be worse off after acceptance than she was before the offer, but she is better off since she will not drown. Hence, Marvin's offer is a *forcing offer*.[2]

According to Robert Nozick, Marvin's proposal is a threat because in the "normal or expected course of events," one aids people in such situations.[3]

But in my opinion Marvin's proposal is a forcing offer, not a threat. Marvin's proposal lacks two essential characteristics of a threat. First, Marvin (as in a forcing offer) has no intent to impose harm or any adverse consequence on Mildred, who is already drowning. Second, if Mildred complied with Marvin's "threat" she would be worse off after accepting Marvin's proposal than before the proposal, when she was drowning. But Mildred, as in a forcing offer, is not worse off after accepting Marvin's offer. On the contrary, she is better off, since she will be saved. Mildred is forced to accept Marvin's proposal, but this is so of a forcing offer as well.

It is true, as Nozick claims, that in our society it is "morally expected" that Marvin would aid Mildred. But that does not mean that Marvin is threatening Mildred. Suppose Marvin and Mildred lived in an exceptionally selfish society where it was not "morally expected" that one aid people such as the drowning swimmer. Marvin's proposal to Mildred is still a forcing offer and, despite the society's moral expectations, is an immoral forcing offer.

The Lecherous Millionaire

A millionaire offers to pay for a child's life-saving operation if the child's mother becomes his mistress for a period.*

Let us assume that the mother is forced to accept the rich man's offer as the lesser evil than her child's death.

* An earlier version of the lecherous millionaire case was described by Daniel Lyons: A lecherous banker tells a poor woman who owes him mortgage payments that if she sleeps with him, he will refrain from foreclosing the mortgage and turning her out in the street. Daniel Lyons, "Welcome Threats and Coercive Offers," *Philosophy* 50 (October 1975): 425–36.

According to some philosophers, such as Theodore Benditt and Joel Feinberg, the millionaire's proposal is a coercive offer because, they argue, the vulnerable mother is unfairly taken advantage of (Benditt), she is forced to do what he wants (Benditt), and the millionaire's purpose is to force her to accede to his desires (Feinberg).[4]

I suggest that the millionaire's proposal is a forcing offer, not a coercive offer, since being forced and being taken advantage of characterize a forcing offer. Also the millionaire does not intend, as in coercion—but not as in a forcing offer—to impose a hardship on the mother if she rejects his offer.

Even if the millionaire's purpose is to force the mother to accept his offer, his offer still is not coercive. If the offer were coercive, she would be worse off after acceptance than before the proposal. But since she accepts the offer, we may assume that she is less badly off, hence better off, than before the proposal, when she could not pay for her child's operation.

Forcing Offer as Just an Offer?

According to Robert Nozick and Michael Taylor, generally, a rational person is willing to have offers made but is not willing to be coerced.[5]

Suppose Irving accepts an atrociously paid job which he needs to feed his family. According to Taylor he is not coerced into acceptance, since he does not regret the proposal's being made. Hence, the employer's proposal is an offer.

I agree that that Irving is not coerced into accepting the employer's proposal. On the one hand, he does not regret the proposal's being made since he is less badly off and hence better off than before the employer made it. Moreover, the employer is not threatening him, so he is therefore not coerced into acceptance.

On the other hand, the employer's offer is relevantly similar to coercion. Here is why:

Although Irving is willing to have this offer made, he is *forced*—as in coercion—to accept a lesser evil (the atrociously paid job) rather than a greater evil, starvation of his family.

Such forcing is not true of nonforcing offers. Hence, I suggest that within the category of offers, *forcing offers* (such as this offer to Irving) should be distinguished as a significantly different kind of offer.

Threat-Offer Distinction

Throughout my analysis of social forcing I have distinguished between threats and offers. But Alan Wertheimer questions the significance of this distinction. He considers the following case: suppose an employer threatens his worker, "Take a pay cut or I'll move my factory." According to Wertheimer, this case indicates that the significance of the distinction between offers and threats can be questioned.

He argues that this threat—like many others—"could be recast as offers." Hence, he questions the importance of the threat-offer distinction. Wertheimer claims that the employer could argue: "I'm not threatening anyone. I hire everyone on a day-to-day basis, so I'm not threatening to fire anyone. Actually, I'm offering to continue to hire this worker only if he accepts a lower wage than I have offered in the past."[6]

My response to Alan Wertheimer: did this employer originally say he was offering this worker only one day's work? If so, he is like the employer who hires workers, such as the migrant laborers who congregate on street corners waiting for offers of a day's work, on a day-to-day basis. *The offers they receive are for one day's work*. Hence, a lower wage offered the next day is a *new offer*.

But suppose in Wertheimer's case, when this worker was hired, he did not receive an offer of only one day's work. In that case, the employer who says, "Accept a wage cut or I'll move my factory abroad" is threatening the worker with harm—the loss of his job.

Hillel Steiner questions the way in which the threat-offer distinction might be made. His view can be illustrated in the following cases:

1. An employer offers Bill a better job than the one he currently has. Bill prefers to accept.

2. A worker, Sharon, is coerced, "Take this dangerous work assignment or I'll fire you."

It is true, as Hillel Steiner writes, that in both offers and threats (as exemplified in the above two cases) "compliance promises to make one better off than non-compliance." Hence, the distinction between offers and threats cannot be made on this ground.[7]

I agree, but the relevant comparison of preferences that distinguishes offers from threats is between the *preferences after accepting the employer's proposal compared with the preferences in the preproposal situation*.

Coerced Sharon would prefer to be back in the preproposal situation when she had a better work assignment. But, when Bill accepts the offer of a better job he would not prefer to be back in the preproposal situation, since now he has a better job.

This preference comparison between offers and threats also holds for a forcing offer.

Larry May and John C. Hughes note that "sexual threats are coercive because they worsen the objective situation the employee finds herself in." They show this concretely in the situation of a secretary "before and after the [sexual] threat has been made (preproposition stage and postproposition stage)."[8]

Broad Interference

According to Broad Interference, the employee is *just unfree* in coercion cases. But in both forcing offer and systemic forcing cases the worker is *just free*. However, as I have argued, in all three strong forcing cases—coercion, forcing offer, and systemic forcing—the workers are *both* free and unfree.

They are free in each of the three strong forcing cases (coercion, forcing offer, and systemic forcing) because no obstacle prevents them from accepting the lesser evil. But in all three cases of strong forcing, they are forced to reject the greater evil. Hence, they are *unfree* to refuse it. Thus, in each of these cases—coercion, forcing offers, and systemic forcing—they are both free and unfree. The fact that workers are forced in all strong forcing cases is what is ignored by Broad Interference philosophers.

Some defenders of the free, that is, capitalist market, such as Milton Friedman, agree with Broad Interference. The workers are *just unfree* in coercion and *just* free in the forcing offer and systemic forcing cases. Hence, my arguments against Broad Interference apply to them as well.

Narrow Interference Critics

According to Narrow Interference, David renders another person, Shirley, unfree to act if and only if he makes it physically impossible for her to act.

However, as I have argued, in all cases of proposal forcing—coercion and forcing offers—the rejection of a proposal is not physically impossible. Yet, Shirley is both free and unfree. She is free because no obstacle prevents her from doing as she does, but she is also unfree (as she would attest) because she is strongly forced to do so.

G. A. Cohen states that "you are free to do what you are forced to do." How can you do something unless you are free to do it? "[Forcing] puts no obstacle in the path of your doing … it."[9]

I too believe that you are free to do whatever you are forced to do, since when you do something, nothing prevents you from doing it. Hence, relative to the absence of an obstacle that prevents you from doing it, you are free to do it. However, as I suggested earlier, you are not only free in all strong forcing cases. You are also unfree.

I suggest that people in these situations would think of themselves as unfree. Let us pay our respects to these workers and say that their unfreedom is more significant than their freedom. To use J. L. Austin's sexist phrase, it is unfreedom that wears the trousers.

Better Jobs?

I have assumed that when a worker is the victim of coercion, his only alternative is a greater or a lesser evil. No better job is available. But according to the economist Milton Friedman my assumption is unrealistic because a worker can usually get a better job. He writes that in a free market (i.e. capitalist) economy, "the employee is protected from coercion by the employer because of other employers for whom he can work."[10] Jan Narveson claims that "nobody is preventing [this worker] ... from moving to a better-paying job."[11]

But I am talking about *rational* workers who have their wits about them. If they could get better jobs they would grab them.

My analysis of freedom has focused primarily on the situation of workers in the United States. In large part, the absence of their freedom is a function of the awful conditions in which they labor. The following glimpse of conditions of workers worldwide gives us an excellent idea of how little freedom workers of the world endure.

> The sad, horrible, heartbreaking way the vast majority of my fellow countrymen and women, as well as their counterparts in most of the rest of the world, are obliged to spend their working lives is seared into my consciousness in an excruciating and unforgettable way.
>
> Whether we speak of the labor of the nation's millions of secretaries and clerical workers, doing tedious work in

front of computer terminals, which gives them permanent muscle pains and chronic headaches, or the tens of thousands of restaurant and garment workers in our large cities, some laboring for 100 hours per week ... or the child care workers, earning just above the minimum wage to take care of other people's children, or the 200 million child laborers worldwide, slaving away in rug-making, farm labor, and prostitution, or the hundreds of millions of unemployed, or even the army of part-time faculty members, the way in which most people spend their working lives is still "sad, horrible, heartbreaking."[12]

Twentieth-Century U.S. Federal Labor Law

U.S. Supreme Court

EMPLOYMENT AT WILL: COPPAGE V. STATE OF KANSAS (1915)

The Supreme Court of Kansas had upheld a statute that made it unlawful for an employer to insist that a worker withdraw from a labor union. However, the U.S. Supreme Court ruled that the statute violated the 14th Amendment:

> The 14th Amendment, in declaring that a state shall not "deprive any person of life, liberty, or property without due process of law," gives to each of these an equal sanction; it recognizes "liberty" and "property" as coexistent human rights, and debars the states from any unwarranted interference with either.

The court stated the doctrine of Employment at Will:

> An employer may discharge his employee for any reason, or for no reason, just as an employee may quit the employment for any reason, or for no reason; that such action on the part of employer or employee, where no obligation is violated, is an essential element of liberty in action; and that one cannot be compelled to give a reason or cause for action for which he may have no specific reason or cause, except, perhaps, a mere whim or prejudice.
>
> Conceding the full right of an individual to join the union, he has no inherent right to do this and remain in the employ of one who is unwilling to employ a union man.*

* U.S. Supreme Court, Coppage v. State of Kansas, 236 U.S. 1 (1915) 236 U.S. 1; T. B. Coppage, Piff. In err., v. State of Kansas No. 48; Submitted October 30, 1914; Decided January 25, 1915.

In the century following the 1915 Coppage decision a number of exceptions have been enacted by federal (and state) laws to the doctrine of Employment at Will. For example, workers cannot be dismissed because of age, race, color, religion, disability, or whistle-blowing. Also, laws have created labor standards such as a minimum wage and overtime pay, occupational health and safety, the right to join a union and engage in collective bargaining.

Federal Laws

The following excerpts from twentieth-century federal labor laws (1914–59) are adapted from *The Congressional Digest*, June–July 1959.[†]

Pre-New Deal Laws (1914–33)

Clayton Act (1914)
This act states that "the labor of a human being is not a commodity or article of commerce" and provides further that "nothing contained in the [federal] antitrust laws shall be construed to forbid the existence and operation of labor ... organizations, ... nor shall such organizations, or the members thereof, be held or construed to be illegal combinations or conspiracies in restraint of trade, under the antitrust laws."

Railway Labor Act (1926)
The Railway Labor Act requires employers to bargain collectively and prohibits discrimination against unions. It applied originally to

[†] Available at http://www.lectlaw.com/files/emp26.htm

interstate railroads and their related undertakings. In 1936, it was amended to include airlines engaged in interstate commerce.

Davis-Bacon Act (1931)

This act requires that contracts for construction entered into by the federal government specify the minimum wages to be paid to persons employed under those contracts.

Norris-LaGuardia Act (1932)

Passed during the last year of the Hoover Administration, this act was the first in a series of laws passed by Congress in the 1930s that gave federal sanction to the right of labor unions to organize and strike, and to use other forms of economic leverage in dealings with management. The law specifically prohibits federal courts from enforcing so-called yellow dog contracts or agreements under which workers promised not to join a union or promised to discontinue membership in one.

In addition, it bars federal courts from issuing restraining orders or injunctions against activities by labor unions and individuals, including the following:

- Joining or organizing a union, or assembling for union purposes; Striking or refusing to work, or advising others to strike or organize;
- Publicizing acts of a labor dispute; and providing lawful legal aid to persons participating in a labor dispute.

New Deal–Era Reforms (1933–38)

National Industrial Recovery Act (1933)

Congress passed the National Industrial Recovery Act (NIRA) at the request of newly inaugurated president Franklin Roosevelt.

The act sought to provide codes of "fair competition" and to fix wages and hours in industries subscribing to such codes.

Title I of the act, providing that all codes of fair competition approved under the act should guarantee the right of employees to collective bargaining without interference or coercion of employees, was deemed unconstitutional by the U.S. Supreme Court in 1935.

The National Labor Relations Act (1935)

By far the most important labor legislation of the 1930s was the National Labor Relations Act (NLRA), more popularly known as the Wagner Act after its sponsor, Sen. Robert F. Wagner (D-NY). This law reenacted previously invalidated labor sections of the NIRA as well as a number of additions.

The NLRA is applicable to all firms and employees in activities affecting interstate commerce with the exception of agricultural laborers, government employees, and those subject to the Railway Labor Act. (These workers were included later.) It guarantees workers the right to organize and join labor movements, to choose representatives and bargain collectively, and to strike.

The National Labor Relations Board (NLRB), originally consisting of three members appointed by the president, was established by the act as an independent federal agency. The NLRB was given power to determine whether a union should be certified to represent particular groups of employees, using such methods as it deemed suitable to reach such a determination, including the holding of a representation election among workers concerned.

Employers are forbidden by the act from engaging in any of five categories of unfair labor practices. Violation of this prohibition could result in the filing of a complaint with the NLRB by a union or employees. After investigation, the NLRB could order the cessation of such practices, reinstatement of a person fired for union activities, the provision of back pay, restoration of seniority, benefits, and other measures.

An NLRB order issued in response to an unfair labor practice complaint was made enforceable by the federal courts.

Among the unfair labor practices forbidden by the act are:

- Dominating or otherwise interfering with formation of a labor union, including the provision of any financial or other support.
- Interfering with or restraining employees engaged in the exercise of their rights to organize and bargain collectively.
- Imposing any special conditions of employment that tended either to encourage or discourage union membership. The law stated, however, that this provision should be construed to prohibit union contracts requiring union membership as a condition of employment in a company—a provision that, in effect, permitted the closed and union shops. (In the former, only pre-existing members of the union could be hired; in the latter, new employees were required to join the union.)
- Discharging or discriminating against an employee because he had given testimony or filed charges under the act.
- Refusing to bargain collectively with unions representing a company's employees.

The NLRA includes no provisions defining or prohibiting as unfair any labor practices by unions. The act served to spur growth of U.S. unionism—from 3,584,000 union members in 1935 to 10,201,000 by 1941, the eve of World War II.

Byrnes Act (1936–38)
The act, amended in 1938, made it a felony to transport any person in interstate commerce who was employed for the purpose of using

force of threats against nonviolent picketing in a labor dispute or against organizing or bargaining efforts.

Walsh-Healey Act (1936)
The act states that workers must be paid not less than the "prevailing minimum wage" normally paid in a locality. It restricts regular working hours to eight hours a day and forty hours a week, with time-and-a-half pay for additional hours; prohibits the employment of convicts and children under eighteen; and establishes sanitation and safety standards.

Fair Labor Standards Act (1938)
Known as the wage-hour law, the act establishes minimum wages and maximum hours for all workers engaged in covered "interstate commerce." (It also prohibits child labor in specified areas of employment. FLSA began applying to federal government workers in 1974.)

Post–World War II Laws (1947–70)

Taft-Hartley Act (1947)
It was not until two years after the close of World War II that the first major modification of the National Labor Relations Act was enacted. In 1947, the Labor-Management Relations Act—also known as the Taft-Hartley Act, after its two sponsors, Sen. Robert A. Taft (R-OH) and Rep. Fred A. Hartley Jr. (R-NJ)—was passed by Congress. Vetoed by President Truman (on the basis that it was antilabor), it was then re-approved over his veto.

The act establishes procedures for delaying or averting so-called national emergency strikes, excludes supervisory employees from coverage of the Wagner Act, prohibits the closed shop altogether and bans closed-shop union hiring halls that discriminate against nonunion members.

Taft-Hartley retains the Wagner Act's basic guarantees of workers' rights to join unions, bargain collectively, and strike and retained the same list of unfair labor practices forbidden to employers. The act also adds a list of unfair labor practices forbidden to unions:

- Restraint or coercion of workers exercising their rights to bargain through representatives of their choosing;
- Coercion of an employer in his choice of persons to represent him in discussions with unions;
- Refusal of unions to bargain collectively;
- Barring a worker from employment because he had been denied union membership for any reason except nonpayment of dues;
- Striking to force an employer or self-employed person to join a union;
- Secondary boycotts;
- Various types of strikes or boycotts involving inter-union conflict or jurisdictional agreements;
- Levying of excessive union initiation fees;
- Certain forms of "featherbedding" (payment for work not actually performed);

The Taft-Hartley Act also contained a number of other provisions:

- Authorization of suits against unions for violations of their economic contracts;
- Authorization of damage suits for economic losses caused by secondary boycotts and certain strikes;
- Relaxation of the Norris-LaGuardia Act to permit injunctions against specified categories of unfair labor practice;

- Establishment of a sixty-day no-strike and no-lockout notice period for any party seeking to cancel an existing collective bargaining agreement;
- A requirement that unions desiring status under the law and recourse to NLRB protection file specified financial reports and documents with the U.S. Department of Labor;
- The abolition of the U.S. Conciliation Service and establishment of the Federal Mediation and Conciliation Service;
- A prohibition against corporate or union contributions or expenditures with respect to elections to any Federal office;
- A reorganization of the NLRB and a limitation on its power;
- A prohibition on strikes against the government;
- The banning of various types of employer payments to union officials.

Landrum-Griffin Act (1959)

The Labor-Management Reporting and Disclosure Act, also known as the Landrum-Griffin Act, makes major additions to the Taft-Hartley Act, including:

- The definition of additional unfair labor practices;
- A ban on organizational or recognition picketing;
- Provisions allowing state labor relations agencies and courts to assume jurisdiction over labor disputes the NLRB declined to consider at the same time prohibiting the NLRB from broadening the categories of cases it would not handle.

Occupational Safety and Health Act (OSHA) (1970)

Congress passed the Occupational Safety and Health Act to ensure that employers provide their workers a place of employment free from recognized hazards to safety and health, such as exposure to toxic chemicals, excessive noise levels, mechanical dangers, heat or cold, stress, or unsanitary conditions.

In order to establish standards for workplace health and safety, the act also created the National Institute for Occupational Safety and Health (NIOSH) as the research institution for the Occupational Safety and Health Administration (OSHA). OSHA is a division of the U.S. Department of Labor that oversees the administration of the act and enforces standards in all fifty states.[‡]

OSHA'S Whistle-blower Program
"Section 11(c) of the Act prohibits any person from discharging or in any manner discriminating against any employee because the employee has exercised rights under the Act.

These rights include complaining to OSHA and seeking an OSHA inspection, participating in an OSHA inspection, and participating or testifying in any proceeding related to an OSHA inspection … "[§]

National Labor Relations Board (NLRB) Decisions

COLLECTIVE BARGAINING OF PRIVATE COLLEGE FACULTY

U. S. Supreme Court: NLRB v. Yeshiva University (1980)
The National Labor Relations Board granted a petition by the Yeshiva faculty union for certification as the bargaining agent for full-time faculty members of certain schools of Yeshiva, a private university. The university opposed the petition on the grounds that faculty

[‡] 29 U.S.C. 651 et seq. 1970.
[§] http://www.osha.gov/dep/oai/whistleblower/index.html.

members are managerial or supervisory personnel and hence not employees within the meaning of the National Labor Relations Act.

The U.S. Supreme Court agreed with the university. The court stated:

> The University's full-time faculty members are managerial employees excluded from the [NLRA] Act's coverage.... Faculty power at Yeshiva's schools extends beyond strictly academic concerns. The faculty at each school make recommendations to the Dean or Director in every case of faculty hiring, tenure, sabbaticals, termination and promotion. Although the final decision is reached by the central administration on the advice of the Dean or Director, the overwhelming majority of faculty recommendations are implemented.**

COLLECTIVE BARGAINING OF PRIVATE COLLEGE STUDENT TEACHING ASSISTANTS

New York University (2000)

In 2000, the National Labor Relations Board held that graduate employees of New York University (a private university) have a right to organize for collective bargaining under the National Labor Relations Act.††

However, in 2004 the NLRB reversed this decision. The board ruled that that graduate students at private universities have no federally protected right to organize. The NLRB held that graduate

** NLRB v. Yeshiva University 444 U.S. 672 (1980).
†† New York University, 332 NLRB (2000) (NYU), http://www.nlrb.gov/nlrb/shared_files/decisions/332/332-111.htm.

students paid to teach or conduct research are not workers but students serving a kind of apprenticeship.[‡‡]

The Personal Responsibility and Work Opportunity Reconciliation Act of 1996

The act is "a comprehensive bipartisan welfare reform plan that will dramatically change the nation's welfare system into one that requires work in exchange for time-limited assistance. The bill contains strong work requirements, a performance bonus to reward states for moving welfare recipients into jobs, state maintenance of effort requirements, comprehensive child support enforcement, and supports for families moving from welfare to work—including increased funding for child care and guaranteed medical coverage."[§§]

[‡‡] Brown University, 342 NLRB (2004). http://www.nlrb.gov/nlrb/shared_files/decisions/342/342-42.htm.

[§§] U.S. Department of Health and Human Services, Administration for Children and Families, fact sheet on the Personal Responsibility and Work Opportunity Reconciliation Act of 1996, http://www.acf.dhhs.gov/programs/ofa/prwora96.htm.

Notes

Introduction

1. All references to the labor market are to the actual labor market in the United States today, not some theoretical construct.

I. The Obstacle Concept of Freedom

1. "Whenever the freedom of some agent or agents is in question, it is always *freedom from some constraint or restriction on, interference with, or barrier to doing, not doing, becoming, or not becoming something* [emphasis added]. Such freedom is thus always *of* something (an agent or agents), *from* something, *to* do, not do, become, or not become something; it is a triadic relation. Taking the format 'x is (is not) free from y to do (not do, become, not become) z,' x ranges over agents, y ranges over such 'preventing conditions' as constraints, restrictions, interferences, and barriers, and z ranges over actions or conditions of character or circumstance. When reference to one of these three terms is missing in such a discussion of freedom, it should be only because the reference is thought to be understood from the context of the discussion." Gerald C. MacCallum Jr., "Negative and

LIBRARY

Positive Freedom," *Philosophical Review* 76, no. 3 (July 1967): 314.

According to MacCallum, the development of this concept resolves the controversy between proponents of what Isaiah Berlin has called "positive" and "negative" freedom. However, that controversy is outside the scope of this work. See Isaiah Berlin, "Two Concepts of Liberty," in *Liberty*, ed. David Miller (New York: Oxford University Press, 1991), 33–57. For a discussion of this controversy, see Hillel Steiner, "Liberty," *Encyclopedia of Ethics*, ed. Lawrence C. Becker and Charlotte B. Becker (New York: Garland Publishing, 1992), 704–7.

2. A journalist "counseled [the women workers who were bringing a suit against Nabisco] to avail themselves of the special diapers that owners of Central Park's horse-drawn carriages had used for their horses." Mark Linder and Ingrid Nygaard, *Void Where Prohibited: Rest Breaks and the Right to Urinate on Company Time* (Ithaca: ILR Press, 1998), 49.

II. Criticism of the Obstacle Concept of Freedom

1. "Broadly speaking . . . a person is unfree to do an action if, and only if, his doing that action is rendered impossible by the action of another person." Hillel Steiner, *An Essay on Rights* (Oxford: Blackwell Publishers, 1994), 8.

According to Thomas Hobbes, however, "FREEDOM . . . may be applied no less to irrational, and inanimate creatures, than to rational" (Thomas Hobbes, *Leviathan* [Oxford: Oxford University Press, 1996], 139).

2. "It is best to start from a conception of freedom that has been central in the tradition of European individualism and liberalism. According to this conception, freedom refers primarily to a condition characterized by the *absence of coercion or constraint imposed by another person*" (emphasis added; P. H. Partridge,

"Freedom," *Encyclopedia of Philosophy*, ed. Paul Edwards [New York: Macmillan and Free Press, 1967], 3:222).

3. David Miller, introduction to *Liberty*, ed. Miller (New York: Oxford University Press, 1991), 17.

4. Robert Nozick, *Anarchy, State, and Utopia* (New York: Basic Books, 1974), 262.

5. G. A. Cohen, *History of Labour and Freedom: Themes from Marx* (New York: Clarendon Press Oxford, 1988), 256.

6. Tim Gray, *Freedom: Issues in Political Theory* (Atlantic Highlands, NJ: Humanities Press International, 1991), 31–41. According to Benn and Weinstein the available choice must not be such that there is no point in doing it, e.g. to cut off one's ears. But I suggest that it is in fact demonstrably true that one is free to cut off one's ears. See S. I. Benn and W. L. Weinstein, "Being Free to Act and Being a Free Man" *Mind* 80, no. 318 (April 1971): 195.

III. Social Forcing

1. Linda Peterson, "Julie Su Savior of Sweatshop Slaves," *Biography Magazine*, December 2000, 87.

2. See Beth Shulman, *The Betrayal of Work* (New York: New Press, 2003), 157, on the lack of benefits for part-time work.

3. Richard Kazis and Richard L. Grossman, *Fear at Work: Job Blackmail, Labor, and the Environment* (New York: Pilgrim Press, 1982), 56.

4. Burton Hall, "Collective Bargaining and Workers' Liberty," in *Moral Rights in the Workplace*, ed. Gertrude Ezorsky (Albany: State University of New York Press, 1987), 162.

5. Shulman, *Betrayal of Work*, 171–72.

6. David Barstow and Lowell Bergman, "A Family's Fortune, a Legacy of Blood and Tears," *New York Times*, January 9, 2003, A1, A20.

7. Shulman, *Betrayal of Work*, 38–39.

8. Ibid., 133–34.

9. See Nancy Holmstrom, "Coercion, Exploitation, and Labor," *American Philosophical Association Newsletter* 94, no. 1 (Fall 1994): 86.

10. See Kim Moody, "Outsourcing, Subcontracting, and Capitalist Restructuring," *New Politics* 10, no. 2, whole no. 38 (Winter 2005): 67, for citation from a Bronfenbrenner and Luce study that surveyed the media for outsourcing announcements during the first quarter of 2004. According to the study, 39 percent of the facilities mentioned were unionized.

11. John J. Sweeney speaking to the American Political Science Association, quoted in Steven Greenhouse, "Unions to Push to Make Organizing Easier," *New York Times*, August 31, 2003, 22.

12. Kate Bronfenbrenner, director of Labor Education Research, School of Industrial and Labor Relations, Cornell University, "Uneasy Terrain: The Impact of Capital Mobility on Workers Wages, and Union Organizing," a report submitted to the U.S. Trade Deficit Review Commission, September 6, 2000.

13. Bob Herbert, "Where The Hogs Come First," *New York Times*, June 15, 2006, A23. For more on Smithfield Foods, see Aaron Sarver, "Processing Pain at Smithfield Foods," *In These Times*, August 2006, 36; Jane Slaughter, "Organizing Meatpacking Hell," *Labor Notes*, August 2006, 1 and 10.

14. Human Rights Watch, "Unfair Advantage: Case Studies of Violations of Workers' Freedom of Association," August 2000, http://www.hrw.org/reports/2000/uslabor/USLBR008-07.htm#P792_193515.

15. Ibid.

16. Steven Greenhouse, "Altering of Worker Time Cards Spurs Growing Number of Suits," *New York Times*, April 4, 2004, A25.

17. Quoted in Rebecca Clarren, "Fields of Poison," *The Nation*, December 29, 2003, 23.

18. Evelyn Nieves, "An Old Story for Migrant Farm Workers," *New York Times*, May 9, 1996, B6.

19. John Bowe, "Nobodies: Does Slavery Exist in America?" *The New Yorker* (April 21, 2003), 107–8.

20. Human Rights Watch, "Adolescent Farmworkers in the United States: Endangerment and Exploitation," *Fingers to the Bone: United States Failure to Protect Child Farmworkers*, June 2000, http://www.hrw.org/reports/2000/frmwrkr/frmwrk006-02.htm#P268_31062.

21. Ibid. Laurence Thomas makes the interesting claim that sexual threats by a woman's supervisor are especially objectionable morally because "they embody the sexist view that if a man has authority over a woman then he has access to her sexually." Laurence Thomas, "On Sexual Offers and Threats," *Moral Rights in the Workplace*, ed. Gertrude Ezorsky (Albany: State University of New York Press, 1987), 124.

22. Human Rights Watch, "Adolescent Farmworkers in the United States."

23. See Human Rights Watch, "Legal Obstacles to U.S. Workers' Exercise of Freedom of Association," *Unfair Advantage Workers' Freedom of Association in the United States under International Human Rights Standards*, August 2000, section on Domestic Workers, for further information on coercion of domestics. http://www.hrw.org/reports/2000/uslabor/USLBR008-08.htm#P1845_445349.

24. Ibid.

25. Kazis and Grossman, *Fear at Work*, 174.

26. David Barstow and Lowell Bergman, "At a Texas Foundry, An Indifference to Life," *New York Times*, January 8, 2003, A1.

27. Peter T. Kilborn, "New Lenders With Huge Fees Thrive on Workers With Debts," *New York Times*, June 18, 1999, A1.

28. Human Rights Watch, "Adolescent Farmworkers in the United States."

29. Zelda Bronstein, "Nowhere Woman," review of Arlie Russell Hochschild and Barbara Ehrenreich, eds., *Global Woman: Nannies, Maids and Sex Workers in the New Economy*, *Dissent* (Spring 2004): 91–95, with reference to Saskia Sassen in book.

30. David Zimmerman, "Coercive Wage Offers," *Philosophy and Public Affairs* 10, no. 2 (Spring 1981): 139.

31. Barry Bearak, "Lives of Workers Held Cheap in Perilous Bangladesh Sweatshops," *New York Times*, April 15, 2001, 12.

32. Joseph Raz, "Liberalism, Autonomy, and the Politics of Neutral Concern," *Midwest Studies in Philosophy*, vol. 7: *Social and Political Philosophy*, ed. Peter A. French, Theodore E. Uehling Jr., and Howard K. Wettstein (Minneapolis: University of Minnesota Press, 1982), 110.

33. Naomi Klein, *No Logo* (New York: Picador, 2000), 352.

34. Gerald Dworkin, *The Theory and Practice of Autonomy* (New York: Cambridge University Press, 1988), 155.

IV. Some Moral Issues of Proposal Forcing

1. Alan Wertheimer, "Coercion and Exploitative Agreements," *American Philosophical Association Newsletters* 94, no. 1, ed. Gertrude Ezorsky (Fall 1994): 80.

2. Jeffrie G. Murphy, *Retribution Reconsidered: More Essays in the Philosophy of Law* (Boston: Kluwer Academic, 1992), 139. See also Alan Wertheimer, *Exploitation* (Princeton: Princeton University Press, 1996), 76, for a thorough examination of the legal issues of unconscionability.

V. Systemic Forcing

1. For a lucid exposition of the Marxist view that the system of capitalist wage labor is itself coercive, exploitative, and immoral, see Nancy Holmstrom's "Coercion, Exploitation, and Labor," *American Philosophical Association Newsletters* 94, no. 1, ed. Gertrude Ezorsky (Fall 1994): 84.
2. Shulman, *Betrayal of Work*, 43.
3. Ibid., 29.
4. Ibid., 2–3.
5. Kim Moody, *Workers in a Lean World* (New York: Verso, 1997), 192.
6. Shulman, *Betrayal of Work*, 30–31.
7. Cited with permission from Chithra Karunakaran's correspondence to me dated August 22, 2005.
8. Lisa Belkin, "A Sick Child Tips the Balance for Parents," *New York Times*, February 29, 2004, job market section.

VI. Criticism of Social Forcing Analysis

1. Frankfurt writes: "First, the customer is *dependent* on the butcher for meat: he cannot readily obtain it from another source. Second, the customer *needs* meat: it is essential either for preventing what he would regard as a significant deterioration of his welfare or for preventing his continuation in what he would regard as an undesirable condition. Third, the butcher *exploits* the customer's dependency and need; he demands for his meat an unfair or improper price. When the first two of these conditions are satisfied, the butcher has the customer in his power. If he then offers meat at an exploitative price, his proposal to refrain from giving the customer meat if the customer does not pay what he asks is a threat." Harry G. Frankfurt, "Coercion and

Moral Responsibility," *The Importance of What We Care About: Philosophical Essays* (New York: Cambridge University Press, 1988), 33.

2. Vinit Haksar, "Coercive Proposals (Rawls and Gandhi)," *Political Theory* 4, no. 1 (1976): 69.

3. Robert Nozick, "Coercion," *Philosophy, Science, and Method: Essays in Honor of Ernest Nagel* (New York: St. Martin's Press, 1969), 449–50. See also Lawrence Crocker, *Positive Liberty* (Hingham, MA: Martinus Nijhoff, 1980), 22–23. Although his example is different—raising the price of fire fighting equipment during a fire—it is relevantly similar to the greedy lifesaver case.

4. Theodore Benditt, "Threats and Offers," *Personalist* 58, no. 4 (October 1977): 384. Joel Feinberg, *Harm to Self: The Moral Limits of the Criminal Law*, vol. 3 (New York: Oxford University Press, 1986), 233.

5. Robert Nozick states that a rational person "would normally be willing to have credible offers made to him, whereas he would not normally be willing to be the recipient of credible threats." Robert Nozick, "Coercion," in *Philosophy, Politics, and Society*, 4th ser., ed. Peter Laslett, W. G. Runciman, and Quentin Skinner (Oxford: Basil Blackwell, 1972), 131. Michael Taylor states: "A rational individual would prefer not to be the recipient of a threat (whether or not he thinks he would comply) whereas he would generally be willing to have offers made to him and would not regret their having been made" (Michael Taylor, *Community, Anarchy, and Liberty* [Cambridge: Cambridge University Press, 1982], 18).

6. Cited with permission from Wertheimer's correspondence to me, n.d. [1990s].

7. Hillel Steiner, "Individual Liberty," *Liberty*, ed. David Miller (New York: Oxford University Press, 1991), 128.

8. Larry May and John C. Hughes, "Is Sexual Harassment Coercive?" *Moral Rights in the Workplace*, ed. Gertrude Ezorsky (Albany: State University of New York Press, 1987), 117. May and Hughes state that "we proceed from the general analysis developed by Robert Nozick, 'Coercion,' *Philosophy, Science and Method*, ed. Morgenbesser, Suppes, and White (New York: St. Martin's Press, 1969). A very large literature has grown out of this analysis. We recommend the essays by Bernard Gert, Michael Bayles, and especially Virginia Held, collected in *NOMOS XIV: Coercion* (New York: Lieber Atherton, 1973)." May and Hughes, "Is Sexual Harassment Coercive?" 138.

9. G. A. Cohen, "Are Disadvantaged Workers Who Take Hazardous Jobs Forced to Take Hazardous Jobs?" *Moral Rights in the Workplace*, ed. Gertrude Ezorsky (Albany: State University of New York Press, 1987), 65.

10. Milton Friedman, "Freedom under Capitalism," *The Libertarian Reader*, ed. Tibor R. Machan (Totowa, NJ: Rowman and Littlefield, 1982), 81.

11. Jan Narveson, "A Puzzle about Economic Justice in Rawls' Theory," *Social Theory and Practice* 4, no. 1 (Fall 1976): 3.

12. Michael Yates, "Braverman and the Class Struggle," *Monthly Review*, January 1999, available at http://www.monthlyreview. org/199yates.htm, quoting Paul Sweezy's preface to Harry Braverman, *Labor and Monopoly Capital* (New York: Monthly Review Press, 1998).

Index

DATE DUE

NOV 1 4 2002			
NOV 1 4 REC'D			
MAY 1 2 2008			
DEC 1 9 REC'D			

GAYLORD

PRINTED IN U.S.A.

HD 5724 .E97 2007

Ezorsky, Gertrude, 1926-

Freedom in the workplace?